Oh, shi*f*t!

for Teens

DISCARD

JENNIFER POWERS

and

MARK TUCKER

Powerhouse, Inc.

Oh, shift! ™ for Teens
Copyright © 2012 Powerhouse, Inc.
www.ohshift.com/teens

Edited by Susan Anglada Bartley, M.Ed.
Back cover photo by Brian McDonnell
Interior drawings by Milena Salieri
Cover design by Ranilo Cabo
Formatting based on concept created by Kent Gustavson

Published by:
Powerhouse, Inc.
Portland, OR
www.powerhouse-publishing.com

Printed in Oregon, USA

ISBN 978-0-9854738-0-8

For Kenyon and Quinten

TABLE OF CONTENTS

Foreword

Adults need to challenge teens' beliefs, hold them accountable, and teach them to build strong, healthy relationships. Teens of today require five things: survival, freedom, power, belonging, and fun. When a particular need is not appropriately met, teens act out; just like any of us might react when we don't get what we want. As adults, we learn skills and techniques to manage these difficult periods. How do we teach these tools to our young people? Well, you're holding the toolbox in your hand.

I've been treating teens and their families for nearly 20 years. When I picked up a copy of *Oh, Shift! for Teens* I thought, "Sh*t, another self-help book written by psychologists who aren't connected to real-life teens." I was wrong.

Mark Tucker is a veteran high school teacher who has more than ten years of direct experience with teens, and Jennifer Powers is an acclaimed author who derives her philosophy from both research and real life experience. As I read their work, I immediately resonated with its direct approach, original style and relevant principles, as it very much parallels my work with teens. I have a no BS approach. As a cowboy from Montana, I'm a little different than your typical mahogany desk, NYC therapist...but I get'er done...and so does this book.

Oh, Shift! for Teens is an amazing step-by-step guide for teens to make serious "shifts" in their own lives; the book places the power back into their hands. The authors remind teenagers that they have a choice in how they're going to react in any given situation. Good choices lead to positive relationships and happier lives. Isn't that what it's all about?

This is a book I will utilize in my practice for years to come.

-Mike Linderman, Licensed Counselor and Author of *The Teen Whisperer: How to Break Through the Silence and Secrecy of Teenage Life*

Preface

We don't have it all figured out, but what we do we want to share. Of course, we were teens once too (back when Lady Gaga was only Baby Gaga-Goo-Goo and when a flip phone was the size of a Razor scooter.) But things have clearly changed since then. That's why we went straight to the experts – YOU, the teens of today, to hear what *you're* experiencing, feeling, thinking and needing. We've heard you and we "get" you. Now we want you to get this...

This book can change your life.
But not in one hour, one day or even one read.
It will show you how to take baby steps towards *shifts* that will collectively make a huge difference.

It will invite you to look at life differently.
It will give you power and control.
It will get you *shift-faced.*

We promise.

Here's the deal. Since its first publication, the principles in *Oh, shift!* have helped thousands of adults change their lives.

Yeah, I believe it, Jen. The principles that you talk about have literally changed *my* life.

Jennifer: Now it's time to share these tools with the teens of today, who could also benefit from taking a good shift.

Mark: You're right! It's not easy being a teen. They're challenged with finding friends, establishing identities, performing well in school, taking on new responsibilities _all the while_ being expected to emerge as functional adults.

Jennifer: Oh man, don't remind me.

Mark: Plus, teens are subjected to a huge amount of social pressure. Keeping up with the latest styles, technology, and trends can be super stressful.

Jennifer: Yeah, that's kind of how it was when I was a teen.

Mark: Yep. And imagine doing all that with the added distraction of devices like smart phones, IPods, and computers.

Jennifer: Ouch! Good point.

Mark: And nowadays the payoff for their efforts looks less and less rewarding. Instead of competing with the other kids for entry level jobs, now young people are competing with unemployed adults and overseas workers. Their futures can look downright scary.

Teens need the life changing tools in *Oh, shift!* now more than ever, Jennifer. So how can they make shifting work for them?

Jennifer: I'm glad you asked, Mark. It simply starts by changing one little letter.

Hmmmm. That reminds me of a story...

One little letter

Year... 1989
Place... Granada, Spain
Lesson...Bueno

I was in my second year of college when I had the opportunity to study abroad in Spain.

My host family was nice. Rich too.

Mama Encarnita was sweeter than sugar and as wide as she was tall. An amazing cook and a lover of red wine, she became my instant bestie.

Jose, the host dad, didn't say much, but when he did he was questioning the "politico Americano" which I knew (or cared) little about. So we were happy to simply say hello in passing at six in the morning when he was waking up for work and I was stumbling in from the never-ending party scene on the streets of Granada.

They had a daughter my age named Rosario, who loved to poke fun at my big Jersey hair and my horrible Spanish accent. Fun stuff.

I wasn't there two weeks when it happened.

The moment that will go down in history.

The story that Encarnita's family will tell every friend, neighbor and exchange student for as long as they walk the earth.

Mama Encarnita thought it would be fun to invite some extended family members to come meet me, so she planned a special dinner. Oh, and it *was* special.

There we were, sixteen of us. Cousins, in-laws, brothers and sisters, Rosario's English teacher Susanna, and Pedro, the tobacco shop owner from across the street.

Dinner was served. The red wine was flowing and the mood became light. Mama Encarnita and her sister Anna made the most delicious dish I had ever put in my mouth; chicken stewed in a rich tomato sauce together with eggplant and capers and a strong dose of fresh garlic. One word: *Yum-o-rama.*

Self-conscious of my weight growing up, I was always hesitant to ask for seconds, especially around strangers. But I figured, when in Spain...EAT.

Soooo, in my best Spanish I asked for more chicken...

"Quiero más polla, por favor."

Silence.

For three seconds.

Then an eruption of laughter so loud they could hear it in New Jersey. Wine and food went flying through noses clear across the table.

The women lost it. Pedro did a sign of the cross and got up to leave the room. Jose had a creepy grin on his face and his sixty-year-old brother Felipe looked aroused.

"What?"

I was definitely on the *outside* of an *inside*.

Rosario's English teacher finally leaned over and let me in.

"Chicken is *pollO* not *pollA*!" she said through a busted gut.

I wasn't surprised. I was, and still am, notorious for making that mistake. Masculine and feminine words just never made sense to me.

"So what? Is it really that funny?"

"Yes, you just said, 'I want more penis, please!'"

Oh what a difference
one little letter can make.

Oh, shift!

Just say it.

"Oh, shi*f*t!"

It's really quite simple.

Change the word that brings you down
to a word that lifts you up.

The difference is one little letter.

And it's a good one… *f*

Go ahead. Slip it in there right
between the "i" and the "t" and
then say it out loud.

Now, believe it or not, for some people that's a challenge.

Babs, one of Jen's fellow New Jersey friends, admitted that it took her great levels of concentration and effort to say the word *with* the f.

Ahhhh, those Jersey girls.

But most people aren't like Babs.

Changing a word is easy. We actually do this all day long.

When talking to children, old people, teachers and parents, we tend to choose the more intelligent-sounding alternatives over our lazy *slanguage*.

"Yeah" becomes *"Yes."*

"What's up?" becomes *"How are you?"*

"Dunno" becomes *"I'm not sure."*

Or we censor our more colorful language and opt for the G-rated version. (Think: *heck, darn, frickin', geez.*)

'Nuff said.

Why do we do that?

The words we choose help us

be what we want to be.

We do it for our parents to be good kids.
We do it for our peers to be good friends.
We do it in class to be good students.
We do it on interviews to be good candidates
We do it for our crushes to be more attractive.

Why stop there?

In the moments of solitude, when no one
is around, you can choose your words so they
create a good impression on your life.

Words give you
power and **control**.

You are given a
blank canvas each day.

Your words are
your paint.

You are if you say you are.
You will if you say you will.

Tell yourself *you suck at math* and you will.
Tell yourself *you'll never get a date*. Done.
Tell yourself *you're always late* and you will be.
Tell yourself *you're fat*. You got it.
Tell yourself *you'll bomb the test*. OK. No problem.

You call it.
It's your choice.
It's your life.

Gym is my least favorite class. I'm not very athletic and I don't like having to dress for it, especially in front of everyone else. I started to feel really anxious and nervous on the days I had gym class. I would say to myself, "I hate this!" "Why do I have to do this?" or, "You suck at sports and everyone knows it."

Then I read somewhere that our words have a lot of power in them and I thought maybe I should start saying different things about gym so I could feel different. I started saying "I like gym." or, "It's kinda fun to get out of class." And, "I'm a pretty good runner." None of these were 100% true, but they weren't completely false either. I just kept saying sentences like these every day before gym and I noticed that my nervousness went away a little bit. I still don't love gym, but at least I don't dread it like I used to. Kinda cool.

Jenna, 14

Yeah, Jenna. YOU'RE kinda cool.

Life is made up of a gazillion choices.

You make hundreds every day, dozens every hour.

Think about it...

What to wear
What to eat
What to say
What to watch
When to study
Who to text
Who to like
Who to call
Who to date
Where to go
How to act
How to feel

Based on the choices you make,
your day will play out one way or another.

Based on how your day goes,
your collective week will be determined.

Based on what kind of week you have,
your month will follow suit.

That flows into years and, of course, life.
You get the picture.

But here's what you may not get...

What you say will influence what you think.

What you think will influence how you feel.

How you feel will influence what you do.

What you do will influence your results.

...Every time.

This is a true domino effect.

Let's say your parents give you additional chores at home but your freedoms and allowance will stay the same.

You choose to **say**...
"Oh, sh*t!"

Which makes you **think**...
This isn't fair. I'm being taken advantage of.

Which makes you **feel**...
Unappreciated, defensive and miserable.

Which makes you **do**...
Interact negatively with your parents, walk around with a scowl on your face and a chip on your shoulder the size of Everest.

Which **results** in...
Your parents giving you an attitude adjustment/
taking privileges away/grounding you.

Dominoooooooooooooo.

Now imagine the same scenario but instead:

You choose to **say**...
"Oh, shift!"

Which makes you **think**...
I am being asked to take on more responsibilities because they trust that I can handle it.

Which makes you **feel**...
Flattered. Happy. Empowered.

Which makes you **do**...
Get along better with your parents, take more initiative and walk with more bounce in your step.

Which **results** in...
Your parents trusting you more and giving you more privileges.

Cool, huh?

Saying "Oh, sh*t!" is useless.

It does nothing for you.
It's a curse.
A purposeless expletive
that leaves you hanging
with no recourse.

Saying "Oh, shift!" is a choice.

It's not mandatory.
It's an option you have
every time something
happens in your life.

When you say "Oh, shift!" you redesign your thoughts, feelings and actions, which will ultimately redesign your life.

Now that's some cool shift.

Attitude Adjustment

Year... 1988
Place... Rock Springs, Wyoming
Lesson...Control

When I was a senior in high school, I worked in the young men's department at the largest clothing store in town. Back then I thought I was a pretty responsible kid – almost always to work on time, friendly to customers, and current on the latest styles. Parents who came in to shop for their teens always asked me for help because they could see I knew what was in fashion.

My sales were GOOD. I was named top weekly salesperson five times since I had started. The store manager must've thought I was a great employee. Who wouldn't? I was quite the superstar.

So imagine how excited I was when the manager position in Young Men's finally opened up. What a score! I was ready to make more money and, at my age, being department manager would totally stroke my ego. Naturally, I was the obvious choice. I mean, who better to head the department than me?

So, when I told my manager that I wanted the job, I did so with confidence, and perhaps a bit of cockiness.

Needless to say, I was shocked when he told me Judy, one of the older women from Lady's Fashion, was getting the position. Judy from Lady's Fashion?! I couldn't believe it. I tried to convince my manager that his decision was completely unfair, but he wouldn't listen.

My sense of entitlement turned to anger. I went home in a fury to mull over the injustice of it all.

I was no dummy; this was clearly a case of ageism. Adults love to undervalue teenagers, assuming they can't handle true responsibility. I felt like I had been mistreated, for no other reason than I was not an "adult".

I'll show them.

The next day I reported to my new boss – *Judy*. I was all attitude. I got pissed off every time she told me what to do. What did she know about teens? What did she know about what *we* were wearing? I gave her as much grief as I could. It felt good to let her know she didn't deserve to be my boss. I could tell I was really getting under her skin.

This went on for weeks.
Day after day I would cop an attitude with Judy.
This finally got me a written warning, but I didn't care. I loved making life miserable for her. She deserved it.

Then one day I was bitching to my friend Andy about my job and how much I hated it. He was immediately confused because he knew how much I had always loved working there. When he asked me what changed, I told him about my plan to make Judy's life hell. Andy casually replied,

"It sounds like you're making YOUR life hell."

I acted cool in the moment but that night I really thought about it. Andy was right. I hated a job I once loved. My sales were down, I didn't talk to anyone, and when I did it was just to piss them off. And I felt terrible about all of it.

What I realized was that my bad attitude wasn't hurting anyone but me.

And that sucked.

After thinking about this for a while and reflecting on the situation, I realized that if my attitude had the power to create this mess, it must have the power to turn it around.

I had control and I took it.

The next day I showed up to work with a *new* attitude. I started treating Judy with respect and kindness.

The transformation was instantaneous.
In Judy AND in me.
Now I was working with somebody who I could talk to, my sales went back up and I enjoyed going to work again.

A couple of days later, Judy pulled me aside to compliment me on my attitude change and how much she appreciated it.
A month later at my yearly review, Judy gave me high performance marks and approved a much appreciated raise.

That experience helped me realize that I can literally TAKE CONTROL of my life by choosing my attitude...and so can you.

Yep.
You.

When you say "Oh, shift!" you will think and feel totally different...

Open-minded, like an optimistic problem solving superhero who's ready for anything.
When you feel that way, you will be unstoppable.
Your actions that follow will be purposeful, driven and
so damn amazing.

Choosing to say "Oh, shift!" gives you an open door.

Options.
A mindset that is intentional.

How?

"Oh, shift!" isn't just an exclamation, it's **a directive.**
The expression TELLS YOU TO DO SOMETHING.

It orders you to shift your perspective so you can react in a way
that **SUPPORTS YOU IN GETTING WHAT YOU WANT.**

Genius.

Get creative.

Write **"Oh, shift!"** on a small piece of paper,
on the back of your hand, on your locker door.
Pin it to your wall or make it your screensaver.

Whisper it to yourself.

Shout it out loud.

Tattoo it on your butt for all we care. (Not until you're 18, of course☺.)

Just be sure to keep this phrase front and center at all times.
You never know when you might need it.

CHOOSE
"Oh, shift!"

OVER
"Oh, sh*t!"

...and watch what happens.

The more
you do
the
better
your
life
will become.

What's all this shift about?

It's about choice.

Shifting lets you design your life

by choosing how you react

to everything that happens in it.

Sparks

Year... 1987
Place... New Jersey
Lesson...Missed opportunity

I remember getting into my very first fender bender. I was driving my souped-up '79 Camaro that had just been painted a perfect shiny maroon. The white pin stripe down the side matched the wide whitewall tires. It was a hot car, and I felt even hotter behind the wheel.

On my way back from the paint and body shop, I stopped on a dime at a red light, but the big 'ol Caddy behind me didn't have the same luck.

T he lady driving the Cadillac slammed into my Camaro with such force she pushed me into the car in front of me. My brand new paint job was more than smudged—at both ends.

It got ugly pretty fast. The only thing bigger than my hair back then was my temper. I was PISSED OFF and I didn't have any qualms about showing it.

I got out of the car screaming at the Cadillac lady who, in my mind, was clearly responsible for this mess.

I laid into her. Ripped her a new one. She screamed right back at me, and our verbal catfight began.

W ell, the Cadillac lady got so mad at me for tearing into her, that when we exchanged contact information she used it to make a phone call to my parents. She told them how awful I was in the way I reacted to the accident.

Needless to say, I was grounded.

Being grounded made me miss going to the senior dance with my yummy crush Jeff Johnson.

O h, I was mad. But technically, I could only be mad at myself. It was *my* reaction to what happened that kept me from going to one of the most important events of my senior year; an event everyone insisted on talking about until graduation.

I could not control what happened (the accident), and that in and of itself would not have gotten me grounded. I could only control how I reacted to the accident, and *that* is what kept me from dancing cheek to cheek with Jeff.

In hindsight, I realized my reaction to that single event could have changed the course of my life. Who knows what sparks could have flown that night between me and Jeff?

If I had kept my mouth shut and handled the car accident with a bit of grace, maybe Jeff and I could've had a beautiful wedding, a honeymoon in Hawaii, and a fairytale life (whatever that is).

You get the point.

It's the little choices that collectively
make up the big picture —

LIFE.

Change your choices,
change your life.

Shifting is like learning how to play golf. (But not as boring.)

How did Tiger Woods get so good? (At golf, that is.)

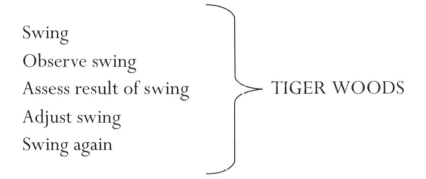

Swing
Observe swing
Assess result of swing } TIGER WOODS
Adjust swing
Swing again

Not complicated. Just good old hard work.

Practice your Shift.
(This is fun.)

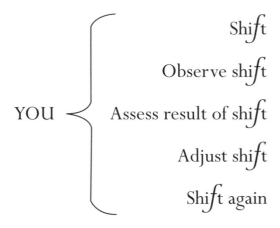

YOU
- Shift
- Observe shift
- Assess result of shift
- Adjust shift
- Shift again

After each shift ask yourself what worked and what didn't,
then adjust as needed and proceed accordingly.*
You *and* your life will get better each time.

*If you skip the observe, assess and adjust part, you will never get better—
you'll get frustrated. Trust us on this one.*

Shi*f*ting builds confidence in who you are and what's possible for you.

Make 1 small shi*f*t and you'll be more confident to make another.

Make 3 small shi*f*ts and you'll develop a pattern.

Make 20 small shi*f*ts and you will feel like a pro.

Then you'll be on your way to taking a BIG shi*f*t.

And who doesn't like that?

Be a shifthead

You can do this.

I used to be super negative all the time. One day, after complaining to my best friend about something, she lost it. She gave me some tough love and basically told me to take responsibility and do something about it. I committed to actively make an effort to be more positive and enjoy myself. Eventually, it worked :)

Alisha, 17

Alisha soooo gets it.

Alisha is a *shifthead.*

Wanna be like Alisha?

The 7 STEPS

to becoming a shifthead.

Step#1 : *Get in the game*

Have you ever played dodgeball?
God I hated that game. I was always the first to get hit.
One day in the 7th grade I got beamed really hard in my ass and everyone laughed. I don't know which stung worse, my ball-burned butt, or my bruised ego. I cried like a baby, right there in front of everyone.

See, getting hit on any other part of my body would have been fine, but in grade school I had a funny - (read: large) shaped butt that kids loved to laugh at.

The thing about dodgeball is that you're supposed to *avoid* getting hit. But eventually you will. Everyone gets hit at some point.

It's kinda like life.

You get pummeled by negative situations and people all day long, and you don't get to choose where or when they hit you.

Sometimes, you will get hit where you are most vulnerable.

And it will hurt.

But it's not getting hit that you are meant to worry about. More importantly, it's how you react when you *do* get hit.

Being a shi*f*thead means you're

on the lookout for the big red rubber balls

being wailed at you from every direction.

You see them coming and you know how to duck, jump, dive and hop at just the right moment to get out of their way before they slam you in the ass.

Getting hit is part of the game, and not always within your control. But how you react when you get hit is always within your control.

As a shi*f*thead, *now* when I play dodgeball and get hit, I have a totally different reaction.

I thank God I can sit down and stop playing that stupid game.

Step#2 : *Be a quitter*

Shi*f*theads quit blaming everything and
everyone for their life being the way it is.
They realize that although it's easier to fault others,
it's clearly not the most powerful way to live.
So they QUIT.

Shi*f*theads quit having pity parties for themselves.
Waste of time. Life's short.
So they QUIT.

Shi*f*theads quit doing what they've always done.
Because they know if they don't, they'll always get
what they've always gotten.
So they QUIT.

Step#3: *Be insistent and consistent*

T o create a shi*f*t that is sustainable, you have to work at choosing your reactions wisely every single day.

Go into this process knowing that trying harder will not necessarily make shi*f*t stick. Trying hard will create shi*f*t in your life, but it's the insistent and consistent effort that'll keep it around.

The journey to becoming a shi*f*thead has a beginning and an ending, but not only one. Each day when you wake up, you begin the process all over again. You get to decide how you will react to everything your day presents to you.

Oh, and you'll slip and backslide for sure.

It's part of the process.

Again, you have the power to choose whether or not you'll get up and keep going.

Did you know you had this much power?

Saaa-weeeeeeeet!

Step #4: *Stay in the moment*

B eing a shifthead means standing in your power to choose your reality, right here right now. Not tomorrow, not next year.

Right now. That's where you have to live if you plan on taking control of your life.

In the NOW.

To shift, you have to be present in the moment to choose your feelings, thoughts and reactions appropriately.

When something negative happens and you react based on what it will mean for your future, you have missed the opportunity to control your present. You have lost your power. You gave it away. Poof.

For example, when you oversleep for an exam and you think about the downward spiral effect it will have on your grade (the future), you miss the opportunity to react appropriately in the moment (the present).

When you feel like your parents are talking down to you and your knee-JERK reaction is to shout at them, your results will be lame at best.

By staying in the moment, you keep the situation in perspective so you can choose your words, thoughts, feelings and actions more rationally. And therefore, more effectively.

Ta-daaa!

Focusing on the future negates the present.

Like Confucius said…

"You must stay in the present
if you want to be powerful there."

Well, if he didn't say that,
he should have.

Step#5: *Raise your pain threshold*

Becoming a shifthead requires you to change, and let's face it, change can be painful.

Many of us stay in a less than ideal situation because we fear the pain associated with change.

It's like when you are hanging out with your friends and one of them starts trashing somebody you think is cool. It would be easier to just do what you've always done and go along with them.

But as a shifthead you are willing to rock that boat by doing something different (ie, standing up for your friend) even if it feels awkward.

Becoming a shifthead will be uncomfortable. It will stretch you. And that's good.

Because **when you stretch you grow.**

Yes, it may be difficult. Change often is. But like anything, the more you shift the easier it will become.

It's a lot like trying to write with your opposite hand. At first attempt you will feel awkward and incompetent. Your tendency will be to put the pen in the other hand where it is comfortable.

But if you **resist that temptation** and you keep writing, **even though it is uncomfortable,** you will eventually begin to improve. You will train yourself to write with a different hand.

You can so *handle* this.

Step#6: *Be a rebel*

S hift heads march to the beat of a different drum. And their friends and loved ones may not *feel the beat*, if ya' know what we mean.

Choosing to react in ways others are not used to may ruffle some feathers. If they can't handle the change, it may require you to break free from the flock you fly with.

Think of that friend, classmate or family member you can always count on to bitch with about anything. He or she may not be thrilled to find out that you no longer aspire to trash the world.

This is tough. But you, fellow shifthead, are tougher.

Like Mom always said, "Tell me who your friends are, and I'll tell you who you are."

Birds of a feather flock together.

You're an eagle now. They choose to remain pigeons.

Fly away pretty bird.

Fly away.

Step #7 : *Be a victor, not a victim*

Our friend Tina, who has been blind from birth, taught us this. She knows the difference and she chooses to be a victor in her life, and ours, every day.

She totally owns it. It's as if Tina was born into the role of shi*f*thead.

But most of us aren't like Tina. You have to choose to be *reborn* into the role of a **victorious** shi*f*thead.

And in doing so you choose to see yourself not as a victim of circumstance but a **conqueror** of all challenges.

You'll never find Tina blaming her reality on the fact that she drew the short straw. Nope. Tina sees every straw as **purposeful** and **positive.**

Tina looks at everything that happens – good or bad – in a way that serves her, not defeats her.

It's possible that Tina has

better sight than most of us.

Shift or get off the pot

Get ready.

I f you bought this book we assume it's because there's some part of your life you want to change.

If someone gave you this book, that person loves you enough to show you that you have lots of options. Go kiss them.

However this book found its way into your hands, it came to you in the form of a gift. Either by yourself or someone else, you have been gifted.

Gifted with the grand opportunity to experience more freedom, choice, friendships, health, happiness, power, success, control, confidence, patience, peace, love, fun, truth.

You name it.

Whatever you're longing for, the principles in this book will show you how to get it.

No shift. You can have it.

Are you ready?

T ake this quickie *Readiness Assessment*. (No pen required)

Count on your fingers how many of these statements you agree with.

o   I am ready to stop blaming everything and everyone for my life being the way it is.

o   I am ready to stop feeling vulnerable, angry, powerless, self-conscious, ignored, patronized, pressured, rejected, defensive, restricted, argumentative, lame, undervalued, unorganized, unlucky, lost, lonely, sad, fat, ugly and tired.

o   I am ready to change the things about myself that don't serve me.

o   I am ready to have a different life experience.

o   I am ready to feel powerful.

How many fingers do you have up?
Five? You're ready.
Less than 5? Don't sweat it. We'll have you convinced you're ready by the end of this section.

Let's take a look at each of these statements to see what we can do to prepare you for the time of your life...

I am ready to stop blaming everything and everyone for my life being the way it is.

Have you ever said the following… ?

"I'd be happy if my **parents** would just stop nagging me."

"School sucks because there are too many **rules**."

"My grades are low because I don't like my **classes**."

"I don't like my classes because my **teachers** are too strict."

"My **friends** don't appreciate me enough."

"I'm stressed because my **schedule** is too busy."

"I am just not a **lucky** person."

"If I had **better clothes** I'd be more popular."

"It's my **brother's** fault."

Etc.

If you've ever used lame excuses like these to
avoid holding yourself accountable for the
outcome of your life, you are normal.

But who wants to be normal?

Normal ≠ Good

Just because something is normal,
doesn't mean it's good. And
   you so deserve to be good.
      Better than good, actually.

         So, take a look at your life.
         All of it.

            What are you blaming others for?
            When will you be ready to stop?

How does NOW grab you?

Own your own shift.

Do yourself a favor.

Stop relying on everyone else to make you feel happy, appreciated or in control.

There is no way you're going to win at this game called life by relying on your herd of scapegoats.

You deserve better than that. The only person you can point your blaming finger at is you. After all, this is *your* life. No one but *you* is responsible for your happiness and success.

You're the boss, applesauce.

Own it.

Next...

I am ready to stop feeling vulnerable, powerless, self-conscious, ignored, angry, patronized, pressured, rejected, defensive, restricted, argumentative, lame, undervalued, unorganized, unlucky, lost, lonely, sad, fat, ugly and tired.

Careful. At first glance, this seems like a no-brainer. Our focus groups of Potential Shiftheads (PSH) thought it was, and they all screamed,
"OF COURSE I AM READY TO STOP FEELING THIS WAY!"
I mean, think about it. Who wouldn't?

But it's not that simple.

In an interview, one PSH told us, *"I don't always remember I have the power to choose. I feel victimized and powerless."*

We loved his honesty, but had to lay down the truth for him, and we'll do the same for you right now.

You feel these feelings because at some level or another they serve you.

Yes. That's right.

You may not think it serves you to live in crappy conditions, but it does. Not necessarily in a good way. But the truth is, we only keep things around (including feelings of inadequacy and powerlessness) if they serve us at some level. In the psychology world they call this "secondary gain."

Check it out.

 I had a student who was failing all his classes and it wasn't looking like he would graduate. I could tell he didn't have many adults he could talk to, so he was eager to talk to me whenever he had the chance. Having grown up in a dysfunctional home myself, I could relate to many of his teen experiences.

One day when I sat down with him to discuss his failing grade, he told me he was angry at his dad because he wouldn't let him live with his mother. At first, I didn't see the connection. After talking a bit more, it was revealed that he was using his performance at school to get what he wanted at home. If he failed, maybe his dad would eventually get frustrated and send him to live with his mom.

Underperforming in school gave him the power to get what he wanted at home.

Yikes!

A lex admitted that he hasn't joined the student council because he doesn't want the responsibility of making important decisions. He said he couldn't stand making a mistake in front of his classmates. *Alex chooses to limit his experiences, and it serves to protect him from embarrassment.*

T amika, although very athletic, admits that she purposely doesn't do well in sports because her group of friends cut on her for being a "jock". *Tamika plays small so her friends will accept her.*

S ienna admitted that she stays with her boyfriend, Cal, even though he's a jerk to her. Breaking up with Cal scares the shift out of her, because if she did she'd definitely lose her popularity. *Staying in a crappy relationship maintains Sienna's popularity.*

QUESTION:

How does it serve you to feel vulnerable, angry, powerless, self-conscious, ignored, patronized, pressured, rejected, defensive, restricted, argumentative, lame, undervalued, unorganized, unlucky, lost, lonely, sad, fat, ugly and tired?

When you answer this question and see how absolutely self-defeating it is to feel this way, then you are one step closer to being ready to shift.

You can't fix what you don't know is broken.

So take some time to do some serious soul searching around that question.

Self-awareness is your friend. The more you know about what makes you tick, the easier it is to fine tune your clock.

Moving on…

I am ready to change the things about myself that don't serve me.

Y es. You are smack dab in the middle of discovering your identity. Perfect. Make *shifting* a part of that process to decide what you want to keep around and what you are ready to let go of.

What parts of you are you ready to change?

Admit it. There are some things about you that could stand some tweaking. It's true for all of us. But if you're going to make these changes you'll want to be prepared because when you become a shi*f*thead you will redefine your current identity. You will change on the inside and those changes will be reflected in your actions on the outside.

You. Will. Change. Are you ready?

You are ready to change when you recognize that the way you are being is not getting you the results you want.

You are ready to change when you give yourself permission to let go of who you are to make room for who you want to be.

You are ready to change when you are willing to say "goodbye" to the old you and "hello" to what's possible.

**Letting go is hard,
but necessary to move forward.**

If you get stuck, think of it not as letting go of something old, but as grabbing on to something new.

Cool.

I am ready to have a different life experience.

Many things will change when you become a shifthead. When you decide you are ready to change you can almost simultaneously expect to have a different life experience. You can't make a change like this and expect the other areas of your life to stay the same.

You will react to the world differently and therefore will have a different experience.

More opportunities, new friends, less stress, more joy, more freedom, a better social life, more confidence and new language are just a few of the changes you can expect.

This means that those who loved being around you before might not now. And those who avoided you before might be magnetically attracted to you.

It also means that the conversations you have will change. Think of all that time you spend talking about how stupid others are or complaining about your day. What will you talk about now?

Your word choices will also change. Phrases like, *I'm lame, Life sucks, What a disaster, and He's an idiot* won't have a place in your vocabulary.

Expect your moods to change.

Are you ready to spend less time feeling down and more time smiling? Sounds like a silly question, but take a moment to answer it, because shifting really *will* turn that frown upside down. Guaranteed.

You can do this.
And make no apologies for it. Own it, just like you've owned the
way you've been up until now.

Every choice you make dictates your life experience.
And when you choose differently,
change is inevitable.

And finally.

Drum roll please...

I am ready to feel powerful.

When we asked our focus groups of PSH's to comment on how powerful they felt, we got this:

(Silence.)

Powerful?
Me?

Heck yeah, you're powerful.

But do you feel powerful?
Yes? Good for you!
No?
There may be a very good reason for that.

Read on, dear friend.

To feel powerful you have to forget everything you were ever told that made you feel inadequate.

Your parents or teachers may have told you something like: *"You'll have to work harder than this if you plan on getting into college."*

Inadequate.

You are told what your body should look like by the Hollywood stars and air-brushed photos in fashion magazines.

Inadequate.

You are constantly compared to your older/younger sibling who does *fill-in-blank* better than you.

Inadequate.

You have to "try out" or "qualify" for nearly every team, club, fraternity or sorority you want to join. And sometimes you don't make the cut.

Inadequate. Inadequate. Inadequate.

The truth is, we were all led to believe that much of what we *do* just isn't enough. And worse yet, much of what we *are* isn't enough (attractive/skinny/popular/athletic/smart).

Ugh.

Few of us were told the truth…

You happen to be perfect just the way you are.

Every bit of you.

Right here, right now you are *doing* and *being* enough.

YOU ARE ENOUGH.

Don't let anyone tell you differently.

They don't know shift.

You are who you are.

YOU.

Accept it.

Embrace it.

Love it.

Feels good, doesn't it?

Here's more good news...

Life

does not

have to be

difficult,

painful,

negative

or a struggle.

You

have

a

choice.

S ure you will have your challenges, but know this:

Life is meant to flow.

Like a leaf floating down a river you roll with the current, the ups and downs, over and around obstacles– going with it, not fighting against it.

So many of us live more like a salmon than a leaf, swimming upstream, against the natural flow. Using all our strength to conquer the greater force that engulfs us.

Why do we do that?

When will we let go and realize that the stream is flowing in the direction it's meant to go, and we are meant to go with it?

Here is the trick.

Explore your upbringing.

What or who led you (or is leading you) to feel, react, think, choose, judge the way you do? It may not be pretty or even fun to dig that deep. But it's so worth it.

L ook at what you are willing to let go of.

What beliefs don't serve you?

What "lessons" or "teachings" will you ditch to make room for new ones?

Do not ignore this step.

If you think you can, think again.

We have *all* been programmed with belief systems that keep us from living a joyful life.

Find yours and call them out.

Then replace them with beliefs, lessons, teachings, thoughts, choices, feelings and reactions that serve you.

Help with this can be found in a good counselor.

Don't be ashamed. Every rock star sees a counselor.

Life can be easy, joyful, painless and juicy delicious... if you let it.

It's all up to you, oh powerful one.

So, now we ask you...

Are you ready?

- *Will you stop blaming others for the things you don't like about your life?*

- *Are you ready to stop feeling powerless?*

- *Are you willing to let go of who you are to embrace who you can be?*

- *Are you prepared to have a different life experience?*

- *Are you ready to be your most powerful YOU?*

If you answered a resounding YES to all of the above then you are ready to join the movement and shi*f*t like a mutha!

Let's do this.

Oh, and be kind with yourself on this journey.

Go easy.

Take your time.

(But not too much, it's slightly limited.)

Get a load of this shift

New concepts to wrap your shifty little head around.

You're not in control of everything

Time... Now
Place... Right here
*Lesson...Control **this***

We are all part of a system called nature. Nature is very unique in that it's one of the few things we don't have to control. Sure we intervene, but it doesn't need us in order to function and sustain itself. That's because if left untouched, everything in nature is in perfect order.

All by itself.

Imagine that.

When things go awry, nature *shifts* to bring things back into harmony.

Our natural environment has exactly what it needs in every moment.

Enter the human,
stage left.

A s part of this system, we have evolved into thinking, rational beings. But that doesn't mean we are no longer a part of the system; it just makes us think we can *control* the system.

We can't.

We are a part of it and not immune to it.

We human types tend to forget that, though. We constantly take actions that go against the flow of nature in an effort to make our lives "better."

If we don't like the way any part of the system is developing and sustaining itself around us, we cut it down, poison it, hunt it, medicate it, extinguish it, attack it, declare war on it, label it dangerous, or simply curse its existence.

And it almost always bites us in the butt.

T hat's so human; going against the natural flow of the system. If we don't think something is good, fair, profitable or convenient, we do whatever it takes to change or control it.

But think about it. How many events happen on earth every day that *don't* seem good, fair, profitable or convenient?

Ever watch the *Discovery* channel where the baby gazelle gets eaten by a lion? The unhatched penguin that freezes to death? What about the tsunamis, hurricanes and tornados that devastate towns and villages in minutes?

Dutch Elm Disease is one of the most destructive plant diseases of the 20th century. The fungus invades the vascular system of an elm and prohibits water movement in the tree. Without water the leaves and branches begin to wilt and eventually the elm dies.

The disease has killed millions of innocent trees and its origin remains an enigma.

This isn't a biology lesson.
This is nature.

It will take its course and leave little room for intervention, and often no explanation.

So how does all this apply to you?

Look at your life.

How many things happen to you that don't seem
good, fair, or convenient?

Exactly, a lot.

How many of these things
can you *really* control?

The things that happen aren't happening
TO you, **FOR** you or **AGAINST** you.

They are just happening.

You are not here to control **what happens**.

Your job is to control **how you react** to what happens.

The way you react to everything that happens
will determine how your life unfolds
from that point on.

A simple illustration.

The state drastically cuts school funding.

The high school cuts most of the electives offered, including the drama program. All that's left to take are required classes.

Brianna, Jeff and Kat are all aspiring actors who find out they will never be able to take Drama at their school again.

Brianna got super pissed since drama was the only thing keeping her in school, and *she quits*.

Jeff, not being a huge opportunist, decides to take a full load of required classes.

Kat chooses to see this as an opportunity. She starts a drama club and appoints herself as club President.

At graduation,
Brianna is nowhere to be found
Jeff did okay,
and Kat has a kick-ass college resume.

The reality was the same for all three people: the drama program got cut. There was nothing any of them could do to control or prevent that from happening.

But each of them had *control over how they reacted* to it. They each reacted in a different way, so they each got different results.

Easy.
Like pie.

OK.

One more time,

because it's important.

Things really don't happen TO you.

T h i n g s   j u s t   h a p p e n .

It's how you react to those things

that gives you control

of your life.

If a positive result is what we want, why do we react so negatively sometimes?

I'm so glad you asked...

A trip to the head

You are head driven.
You live in your head and you go there for approval, rationale, decisions and, of course, your reactions.

In your head you decide how you will react to everything that happens.

YOU have a choice.

But here's the thing…

Two people live in your head and they are both **YOU.**

Allow me to introduce **YOU**
to your Ego and your Self.

Your Ego is your dark side.

Because it is dark,

The Ego thrives and feeds on pain and struggle.

The fiend, bully, troll, brute. The devil, if you will.

It longs for struggle, challenge and upset.

Looks for it. Fights for it. Feeds off of it.

Actually, your Ego is happiest when it is miserable and in pain.

Funny little bugger.

Your Self is your light side.

Because it is light,
The Self naturally sees the bright side of things.

The angel, peacemaker, light seeker. The buddha, if you will.

It wants to be happy. It lives for joy and peace.

And, when it can get a word in edgewise, it fights for it.

T he Ego and the Self (as I call them) are the two parts of each of us. Forget what these words mean in their psychological context. Just picture the Ego on your left shoulder and the Self on the right, whispering into your opposing ears.

Every time something happens in your life, a power struggle between your Ego and your Self ensues.

In your head there is a mental boxing match between the two opposing parts of you.

Your Ego fights for a reaction that involves struggle, pain and emotional destruction; and your Self fights hard for a reaction that results in joy, peace and freedom.

Back and forth they go.

They each have a voice, and they each want to be heard.

The less obvious problem is that too many of us let our Ego win.

In our culture the Ego has a louder voice, more influence and power. As a result, we have a tendency to default to a negative, painful reaction because that's the way our Ego likes it.

Casc in point...

I accidentally cut someone off on the freeway the other day. Looking back in my rear view mirror, I can tell you that the finger gesturc the guy flipped me was NOT a *thumbs up*.

His knee-JERK reaction came straight from his Ego. His Self was willing and able to react in a way that was less emotionally disruptive, but the guy let his Ego snuff it out. When I accidentally cut him off, he had a choice to make: react from Self or Ego?

He clearly chose Ego.

T hink about the last time something unpleasant happened.

What was your knee-JERK reaction?

It's ok. You can admit it.

I do.

When things don't go my way, my Ego tries to shout the loudest. And to be honest, it sometimes wins.

This happens to the best of us.

That's because we've got human blood running through our veins. And we humans are far from perfect.

But we *are* malleable.

Whew.

How did our Ego get such a loud voice?

I'll tell you how.

The same way we came to believe we were so inadequate.

Our experience and upbringing.

The last several generations have lived through, heard about, and read endless stories of struggle, pain and misfortune. *(Think: natural disasters, drugs, homelessness, wars, race inequality, poverty, obesity, crime and animal cruelty.)*

As a result of our experience and education, we were literally hardwired to believe that pain, struggle and hardship are the status quo.

Sure, we have been given many opportunities. But think about it, how many of those opportunities came without pain, struggle or hardship?

Aren't we taught that soldiers FIGHT and DIE for our freedom? Don't we often have to SACRIFICE one thing for another? Isn't the saying "No pain, no gain"?

All of this programming has trained our very dark Ego to believe it's in charge and able to control our every reaction. This tends to make our knee-JERK reaction to even minor events, flaws or setbacks **Ego-driven by default.**

For example, when I look in the mirror, my knee-JERK reaction is not my Self saying, "You are so good-looking." Instead, it's usually my Ego turning me around, making a disgusted face and saying something like, "Fat ass!"

You get my drift. I know you do.

 Yeah, I know what you mean. My freshman year English professor was impressed by my creative writing skills and told me she thought I could write a book. My Ego went into over-drive.

"You can't do this. It's too difficult to figure out the process of publishing a book. Don't be ridiculous!"

My Ego's voice was so loud. Looking back on that, I realize I was listening to only one side of me.

Arghh!

Have you ever met really nice, happy people and wondered how they got to be that way?

It's not that they don't have an Ego. They do. The difference is that they don't let it have as much influence, voice and strength. They snuff the Ego's voice out. Resist its temptation. Ignore its desires. Shut it down so they can let their Self's voice come through louder and clearer.

Like you, they have a choice.

They choose joy and peace over sadness and pain.

They choose positivity over negativity.

They choose light over dark.

They choose silver lining over gloomy clouds.

They choose.

Same goes for the Negative Nellie Naysayers. They have a choice and they choose to let their Ego control their reactions. In other words, they react in ways that cause them pain and emotional destruction.

They too have a Self, but they choose to ignore it *and* its wishes to react in a way that is peaceful and harmonious.

So that begs the question...

When something crappy happens in your life,
which one typically controls *your* reactions?

□ EGO
□ SELF

(Check one and be honest. No one is looking.)

The trick to being a shifthead

is to give your Self more power than your Ego.

In order to undo years of programming, your Self has to be stronger, more tenacious, tireless, adamant, consistent, almost obsessive compulsive until the Ego backs down and shuts up.

It sounds more difficult than it is, but then again—you've got this whole book to show you the way.

Rock it out.

A conversation between
two pieces of shi*f*t.

Dearest Ego,

You are so overpowering all the time. Why do you keep snuffing me out?

With joy,

Self

```
Yo Self:

If I let go of my incessant search for ways to
suffer, then what the hell would I do all day?
And anyway, why don't you just try and stop me,
you big sissy.

With pain,

Ego
```

Dear Ego:

Here's the thing. For some reason I have let you overpower me and it seems like I am now numb to the effects. It feels like I have been asleep, like when I sit on my foot for too long and it gets all numb. But every once in a while, when I fight hard for happiness and win the power struggle, I start to feel alive and get that tingly feeling. And it feels good.

In that moment, if I am not careful you will sit on me again and put me back to sleep. That's why I have to keep moving. I will not continue to play small so you can feel big. I will keep fighting and you will no longer overpower me.

I will consciously and consistently look for ways to be stronger than you. And no matter how much you fight, or how loud you scream, I will scream louder because I deserve to be heard.

Your constant complaining and negative chatter will be missed at first, but after a while I'll get used to hearing the sound of my own sweet voice saying, "Oh, shift!"

With joy,

Self

P.S. I still love you.

Q.

What if I try to shut my Ego up but I can't? Sometimes I am so angry I can't see straight!

A.

So you are angry, seeing red and feeling like you're gonna explode. Don't do anything. Just observe yourself in that moment of fiery-red fury. Examine the presence of your Ego and its attempt to fuel your pain. Remember, it lives for pain and suffering and it's not ashamed to fight for it. Like a bulldog, it clamps its jaws into any opportunity it has to roll around in pure misery.

Be with that for a moment. Look at the Ego in all of its disgusting glory and recognize that it's only one part of you.

Not the whole you, but part of you.

Honor it. Observe it.

Be gentle and patient with yourself.

This is a process of self-discovery and an unfolding of a new you. Sometimes we try to skip this moment of simple examination. But you'll be so much more effective when you allow space for it. Your awareness will grow, and you will be an expert on the subject of YOU.

The more you know about anything, the better prepared you are to deal with it.

Why take a shift?

Cause it feels soooo good.

My non-existent sex life was suddenly the newest cake that the "mean girls" could not wait to get their hands on. The second the rumor hit my ears I felt like I'd actually been nailed in the gut.
Gossip sucks.
I used to let it bother me for weeks or until the rumor died out. But now I try to look at it differently. In this case, I just considered the source and figured if people are gossiping about me it's probably because their life isn't quite interesting enough. So even though the gossip still hurts, I can get over it faster.

Risa, 18

Every shift, no matter how big or how small,
will give you control over your feelings.

Every shift will contribute to your
physical health and well-being.

Every shift will greatly benefit
your social experience.

Every shift will affect the lives
of those around you.

Every shift will redefine
your experience on an
emotional,
physical,
social
and
global
level.

Yes, global.

Emotionally

When you shift, you take charge of your emotions and own them. You stop blaming other people and circumstances for your feelings.

You stand in your power
by holding yourself accountable for your own reality.

With every shift you are molding your emotions and exercising your power of choice. You choose your feelings instead of letting *them* choose *you* based on circumstances that are out of your control.

When you shift you
redefine the feelings
that will ultimately
redefine your reality.

Shifting means choosing your feelings.

When something happens that makes you feel crappy, who's responsible for you feeling that way?

Did you know that when you let someone or something determine your emotions, you are serving up your power to them on a platter? Giving it away.

It's not their fault. They don't *take* your power.

You *give* it to them.

Your emotional state is decided by you.
And your reality is determined by the way
you choose to react to the situations or people
that show up in your life.

What people say or do is what they say or do. That's it. You can't control them. But you *can* control how you react to them.

We often forget this.

M any of us are happy to take the victim role, whining that this person or that circumstance ruined our day, our week, or our life.

That's "Bull-Shi*f*t!"

No *one* or no *thing* is responsible for any part of your reality. Only you.

The way you react to the events that happen in your life will determine how you *experience* life.

No *thing*,

no *event*,

no *person*
has the power
to make you feel:
vulnerable, angry, powerless,
self-conscious, ignored,
patronized, pressured,
rejected, defensive, restricted,
argumentative, lame,
undervalued, unorganized,
unlucky, lost, lonely, sad, fat,
ugly and tired.

Only you.
It's your choice.

This is YOUR SHI*f*T!

Get it?
Got it?
Good.

My dad likes to get on my nerves. He drives me crazy. A perfect example is when he moved us to a new apartment much further away from my school without even considering how it would affect me. I had to take a two hour bus ride to his work every day after school, just so he didn't have to use his gas to drive ten minutes to come pick me up. We would get home after dark every night. Last Thursday, I was supposed to go to my mom's house and my dad told me I wasn't allowed to go until I cleaned the entire back yard. I told him I couldn't do it because it was dark. He snapped and screamed at me. He said some pretty hurtful things. We yelled at each other for like twenty minutes before I stormed off in a rage. This happens nearly every time my dad and I are around each other. How am I supposed to control my emotions when he has all the power?

Aidyn, 17

Correction. He doesn't have ALL the power.

He may have *some* of the power -maybe even *most* of the power over your circumstances- but you have the power over how you react and feel.

Try this, Aidyn:
When your father makes his next "unreasonable" demand, take a moment to decide which reaction will serve you best.
Guaranteed you'll feel like a superstar quarterback that just made the game-winning pass.

Touchdown!

How much time do you spend

before deciding how to react to the people and events
that show up *(or throw up)* in your life?

Inquiring minds want to know.

Physically

When you shift you contribute to your physical well-being. You control the rate of your heart and the pressure of your blood pumping through your veins. You manage your breath and allow it to feed you oxygen, energy and health.

When you shift you redefine how your mind will affect your body.

It is a decision, and it's yours to make. In every moment you get to decide how you will *let* your body feel.

Will you let your mind go awry and have your body react accordingly, sucking the air right out of your lungs? Or will you manage those thoughts so that your body gets the steady flow of air it needs to maintain a healthy state?

It doesn't take a genius to know that constant fluctuations of heart rate, blood pressure and breathing do not make a healthy person.

 My good friend Dina works in a doctor's office and her mother loves to call her and talk about all the crap that's going on in her life and the world.

This drives Dina crazy.

I asked her to do some research to see what effect these annoying phone calls had on her physical health.

Dina took her resting blood pressure before and after receiving a call from her mother on three separate occasions.

The effects of the annoying phone calls on Dina's body?

BEFORE THE CALL:
Average Blood Pressure: 120/60
(that's good)

AFTER THE CALL:
Average Blood Pressure: 140/87
(that's not so good)

Now, I'm no doctor, but come on.
With a mother like that, who needs terrorism?

Once Dina realized she had a choice, she was able to shift the way
she reacted to her mother. She decided she was no longer
going to be a victim of her mother's toxic effects.
As a result, her blood pressure is
a solid 120/60 before *and* after the call.

Shifting can help you manage your health by controlling the way
you react to life's little annoyances.

Socially

Apart from the inner workings of YOU, there is the external influence that shi*f*ting has on others.

When you shi*f*t, you redefine yourself on a social level.

How?

Your reactions to life and happenstance will cause others to define you in one way or another. That usually translates into:

I like you **or** *I don't like you.*
I want to be around you **or** *I want to avoid you.*
I want to give you opportunities **or** *I don't want to*
And so on.

How you show up determines who (and what) you will attract into your experience.

You'll want to pay close attention to this, because this is the really important part. So important, in fact, that some people call it the *SECRET* to making all your dreams come true. We just call it pure awesomeness.

Here's how it goes.

Y ou can control every aspect of your life experience by simply controlling the type of energy (aka: words, thoughts, attitude, mentality) you put out to the world.

You may have heard some of these familiar statements:

Like attracts like.

What you think about you bring about.

What you focus on expands.

What you put out you get back.

This is all good stuff (and true), but let us simplify it even further.

YOU ARE A HUGE, SUPER-POWERFUL MAGNET.

Each moment of every day you get to decide what you want to attract into your life.

If you show up with your Ego on your sleeve you will attract others just like you. So you'll end up surrounded by Negative Nellies and Ego-driven eggheads that will pull you down.

If, however, you stand in the light and look for ways to consistently view things from a positive perspective, positive people will be drawn to you.

These positive people will (obviously) have positive effects on you. They will lift you up and present opportunities that will ultimately make up your life experience.

How you show up in life will very much determine how your life will unfold, simply based on who or what you attract into your experience.

Now that's some damn good shi*f*t.

Be cool

Year... 1986
Place... Rock Springs, Wyoming
Lesson...Bullies suck

One day in high school, a group of us were heading towards the locker room after gym class. A couple of kids must've thought it would be funny to pull down this guy Devin's shorts. Devin was a slow, skinny, quiet kid, who got picked on because he was an easy target.

The two boys snuck up behind him and yanked his shorts down. A prank like that was sure to get plenty of laughs, while at the same time humiliating Devin.

I'm glad to say that my sense of decency kicked in, and before I knew it I was screaming at the kids for what they'd done. I shouted that if they wanted to mess with somebody, they should mess with me.

The irony was that I weighed about 100 pounds soaking wet and couldn't punch my way out of a paper bag.

But that wasn't the point.

The point was that it's not cool to pick on people who are weaker than you. That may not have been a message that those bullies liked, but that was okay, since I wasn't looking to be friends with them. I was more interested in being friends with friendly, positive people; and in order to do that, *I* needed to be friendly and positive.

When I think about the people I hung out with when I was a teen, it's no surprise that they were kids who supported me and built me up. Having friends like that was way more fun, not to mention that it was great for my self-confidence.

As for Devin, he rarely got picked on after that.

Go figure.

Shi*f*ting
is
not
all
about
YOU.

Globally

You can change the world.

With every shift you take, you will contribute an amazing, positive, radiant, on-fire energy that the world very much needs right now.

> By shifting on the inside,
> you can positively affect
> everything and everyone
> on the outside.

You don't have to take our word for it. A simple 5-minute experiment will prove this.

The next time you're walking down the street, in the park, in your school or in a shopping mall, think of something that makes you happy.

Then let your facial expression reflect that feeling.

You will probably smile. Your eyes will light up, your forehead will unfurl and your walk will take a different stride.

Your shoulders will relax and your breathing will change.

N ow, make eye contact with the people in your sur-
roundings, and observe *their* reaction to *you*.

Watch what happens.

People will feed off your positive energy. Their eye contact
will be longer. They will smile back. You may even get ap-
proached more often.

Why?

Because you've given them a gift; and as a result they will *feel*
different. And you will see that difference on the outside—
through their actions.

What you won't see is the difference you are making on the
inside of each person and the collective world. By simply radiating
a mentality that encourages, elevates and energizes, you are
changing people. You are changing the world by giving people
what they very much need...

Good vibrations.

Mmmm. Delish.

Q. If there are so many benefits to shifting, why isn't everyone doing it?

A. For the same reason we're not all Yale graduates. Some people don't want to work that hard. Some have really thick heads that keep them from seeing the benefits.

Don't worry about them. You've got a job to do, now go do it you fabulous little shifthead. We're rooting for ya every step of the way.

You are going to be amazing.

And gorgeous too.

Shift happens

Actually, it doesn't.

F or shift to happen there are a few **prerequisites** that must be met first.

Trying to shift before doing these would be like trying to put your pants on before your underwear.

It just won't work.

You could do it, but it would be very uncomfortable.

Awkward even.

Before you shift,
you have to
ADMIT,
COMMIT
and
SUBMIT.

Admit

To be a shifthead you have to admit that
the way you're showing up in life
could stand some changing.

It's OK.

Admit it.

The first step in the self-development process is to become aware of the role you're playing in your own life.

By taking a good hard look, you'll identify the areas that could benefit from some tweaking.

This was pivotal for Amy, who was, well…shall we say, "unaware."

Her biggest issue was that she couldn't figure out why she didn't have many friends, and why she couldn't keep the few she did have.

The truth was, Amy's sarcastic (albeit witty) ways of reacting to the world were repelling people like a bottle of OFF repels a campground mosquito. She was stinky, and no one wanted any part of her.

At first, Amy was perfectly happy to blame everyone else:

> *"They're not intelligent enough*
> *to get my humor."*

She also tried to play the authenticity card:

> *"I want to stay true to myself and not*
> *bend to anyone else's expectations."*

And of course, she was fine with attributing this part of her to some external source that made it impossible to change:

> *"I get my wit and sarcasm from my*
> *father. I was born this way. There is*
> *no way to get rid of it."*

my had two options (you always have at least two).

OPTION #1:

Amy could continue to blame everyone and their brother for not having friends. In other words, she could take *zero* responsibility for her life being the way it was.

OR

OPTION #2:

She could take responsibility for the fact that she is playing the starring role in her reality. She could admit that how she was reacting and responding to people was the sole reason she had no friends.

Lucky for her,
she chose
Door #2

S he put on her investigative hat and set out to do a little research.

She picked three people she knew who had lots of
friends and observed how they were "being". Then
she observed how *she* was "being" and compared notes. The differ-
ences were dramatic.

Amy realized that the way she was reacting to the world, the
way she was "showing up," was a direct cause of her friendless
state of affairs.

> The way she was "being" was
> not working for her, no mat-
> ter how hard she tried to
> convince herself it was.

Through tenacity and a desire to change her life, she got to a
point where she was willing to take responsibility.

She was finally
willing to

admit

that

she

was

the

reason

she had
no friends.

When she did, it was ugly and uncomfortable. It was oh so difficult to admit that she didn't have it all figured out. But once Amy admitted she was responsible for her life being the way it was, she was one step closer to fixing it.

And, guess what?

Amy has friends now. Lots of them, actually.

But if it weren't for admitting that she needed to do something different she could not have made some very important changes in her life to get the results she very much wanted...and deserved.

Mega, super, turbo-charged.

If you want to fix anything, you have to first recognize what's not working.

Do some self-observation.
Observe your reactions and your results.

Be with them.

Criticize them and examine how they
currently define your life.
Then ask yourself if they are getting
you the results you want.
If not, admit it.

Out loud, say these words…

"I admit
that if I want to
change my
Reality
I must start by
changing my
Reactions."

If

R = R

(Reactions = Reality)

then

CR = CR

(Crappy Reactions = Crappy Reality)

therefore

PR = PR

(Positive Reactions = Positive Reality)

It's mathematically sound.
We rest our case.

Commit

Commit to change what
is not working.

If you want to be a shifthead, a certain amount
of commitment is required —for no other reason than
it might get tough.

And when the
going gets
tough...

Right here, right now
make a commitment to yourself that
you are in this for keeps.

Here's why.

Throughout this process you will be tempted to turn back,
give up, surrender to your old ways and settle for your old reality.

But know this:

Your chances of successfully becoming
a shifthead are 1000x more probable
if you make a commitment.

That's why we sign contracts.
To get buy in.
To make sure everybody follows through on what they agreed.

And it works.

So, say it out loud.
                    Tell a friend.
          Write it down.

Do something that will keep you committed to making these necessary changes in the way you react to life.

Committing doesn't mean there's no room for failure.
If it did, our divorce rate wouldn't be at 50%.
It does, however, set you up with a more powerful mindset.

So again, be gentle with yourself.

This isn't life or death we're dealing with here…just life.

My commitment

Zoe
Age 18

I made a commitment recently. My good friend Kristen and I are like sisters, but sometimes she acts in ways that really get under my skin.

I found myself venting about her way too often. A couple of weeks ago I was at it again. I was parked at a drive-thru with a couple of friends ordering tacos, and the whole time I was complaining about Kristen. I was in a foul mood - it seemed

the more I complained about her, the more upset I felt.

I looked at my friends and realized that they weren't even listening to what I was saying. Why should they? They had heard it all a million times. It embarrassed me to discover that I had become such a drone of complaints.

Before passing out the tacos, I declared to my friends that from now on I was going to stop complaining about Kirsten.

Just saying it out loud made me feel better.

It seems half the reason I was so upset was that I felt bad about what I was saying. Once I stopped the cycle, I felt a lot better.

Right on, Zoe.

Submit

Submit to the process.
Surrender your Ego.
Trust your Self.

Sometimes you need to give your power away in order to get it back.

T his is one of those times.

When you submit to this shifting process, at first you may feel like you have lost control – given in, settled.

Au contraire mon frère!

That is your beloved Ego speaking.

Remember, the Ego likes pain and struggle, and it's not fond of you discovering ways to take those feelings away.

Your Ego is no dummy. It knows that shifting the way you react to life will reduce struggle and relieve pain. And it just can't have that.

So it will fight. Hard.

Whenever you feel resistance to shifting, that's your Ego fighting to be heard.

Point your finger at it and say:

"Adios Amigo!
There's a new sheriff in town.
Pain and suffering
have now been outlawed."

Then get your guns out, remove the safety, aim right between the eyes and say, "Oh, shi*f*t!" Then say it again. And again.

Blow holes in it until it drops to its knees.

Now, your Ego isn't just going to take that once and say, *"Sayonara!"* It will always be the other part of you. You just have to keep shooting it down. The yin and the yang must co-exist. What would a hill be without a valley? Flatlined.

And that's what *you* will have to be before you get to stop working at this. There is no arrival where you get to say, "Ok. I'm done."

Don't worry. It will get easier as you continue to practice this. But there will be times when you'll have to be on your guard with your gun out of the holster.

Sharp shootin'.

So Jen, how does *your* Ego show up?

Man, when I am having an *Ego-Flare-Up,* I can feel it in my core. It's the worst when I don't like the way someone is acting. The first thing my Ego wants to do is start bitching about it. You know how it goes…

"She must think the world revolves around her. Doesn't she know it's rude to show up ten minutes late to everything?" or, "God, he's such an ignorant jerk. How could he say that in front of everyone?"

Mark: So then what does your Ego do?

Jen: My Ego rips into them, and it's all in the name of pain. It loves to roll around in the misery caused by other people.

My Self, on the other hand, just wants to accept those people for how they really are. Celebrate them and their unique individuality. Allowing their positive attributes to have positive effects on me and my experience.

And yes, it's tough.

I have to consistently work at shooting my Ego down to let my Self shine its light. And when I do, it's so damn bright I need shades!

Mark: Amazing.

Submitting to the process means

trusting that your Self will lead you to joy.

Every effort you put forth.
  Every time you shoot down the Ego
    and let the Self sing its song,
      you are creating a momentum
        that will push you forward.

          YES!
          Forward.
            That's where you're heading.

              To a place where flowers are
              always in bloom and
                the air smells sweet.

A place where you can experience life
as it's meant to be lived—
in a state of happiness,
positivity and f in peace.

              And arriving there is so possible
              once you know how to apply...

The f'in shift

This is how you do it.

T hink for a moment about the past five days.

How many crappy situations did you have to deal with? Big or small.

Consider them all.

Now think about your best friend, teacher, classmate, parents, siblings, your coach and the cashier at McDonald's.

How many did they face?

Think for a moment about the last hour.

At this very moment.

What are you freaking out about?

The possibilities are endless. There's no shortage of things for us to feel crappy about. Actually, there are about as many crappy situations as there are calories in a Cinnabon.

Crunch the freaking numbers...

Depending on what your mother is like or how much you were teased in grade school, you arrive to your teen years with your own set of issues.

X

Multiply that by the amount of different energy sucking people and situations your life presents you with daily.

Combine that with whether or not you use social networking, are neurotic, eat meat, exercise or have a job.

And you've got an UNLIMITED amount of scenarios and situations that a standard approach to shifting just won't cover.

That said, you might be surprised to learn that Omar from Texas who didn't get invited to a party could shift his situation the same way Carla in New York, who just got dumped by her boyfriend would.

Truth is, we would tell Omar and Carla how to shift the same way we would tell you...

Go *f* yourself

To f yourself you

use the f in shift to:

reframe a crappy situation

so you can
take control of your reactions

and therefore
take control of your life.

Check it out...

The *f*in shift represents

*f*LIP, *f*IND or *f*REAK

*f*LIP

means to turn the situation on its head so you can look at it from a completely different angle. These are catch-alls that work for your everyday standard crappy situations. It requires some thought, but less than the others.

*f*IND

means to seek something that you are not readily seeing. When you find it, your perspective will change. A bit more effort and thought needed here, but so worth it.

*f*REAK

means to do something different, odd or irregular. You know, like a freak. Do not underestimate the power of these. They work wonders when you are in a situation that elevates your emotions and makes you feel like you're going to bust a vein. Life savers for sure...and fun too.

These are your *f*'in strategies.

These strategies will help you improve your
situation by shifting your perspective.

They help you react
in a way that serves you.

They help you avoid unnecessary pain,
physical and mental stress, arguments and broken hearts.

They help bring
peace, harmony and joy to your life.

They help you
take your power back.

They help you control
the outcome of your life.

It's like a menu of
f'in solutions.

Here's what you do when you come
face-to-face with a crappy situation.

1

Observe your knee-JERK reaction.
That's right. Just observe it. Notice how your
Ego wants you to react. Notice how you feel.
Then **resist** going there.
You've got better plans for your life.

2

Say "Oh, shift!" Really, say it. This won't work if you
don't say it. Hence the title of this book.

3

Choose ONE *f* in strategy from the chart on page 167 to
reframe your crappy situation. Depending on
your mood, the scene, or how much thinking you
want to do, choose the one that feels best. For
example, choose to *flip your focus* or *find the root*.
One is all you need.

4

Ask   yourself the corresponding question from the chart. Start with the one provided or get crazy and think of your own. Either way, it's gotta be a good question. Powerful. Thought-provoking. Definitely shift-worthy.

Note: Crafting good questions takes some practice. Spend time and have patience.

5

Answer   the question.
Do not take this one lightly. This is where the shift happens. Your Ego will fight this. Find your Self and let it sing.

6

Feel   the shift. Love the **result.**

Here are the goods...

*f*LIP	*f*LIP the focus	What is abundant here?
	*f*LIP your belief/opinion	What belief or opinion would serve me better?
	*f*LIP your feelings	How do I deserve to feel?
	*f*LIP your expectations	What good can come from this?
*f*IND	*f*IND the message	How does this fit into the bigger picture?
	*f*IND a reason	Why did this *need* to happen?
	*f*IND the benefit	How could this actually benefit me?
	*f*IND something nice to say	Whom or what can I compliment or say something nice to?
	*f*IND something to be grateful for	What about this situation can I be grateful for?
	*f*IND the root	What is actually upsetting me?
	*f*IND the truth	What information am I lacking?
	*f*IND the opportunity	What can I turn this into?
*f*REAK	Imitate Buddha, Jesus or any other great one.	What would He/She do?
	Laugh at the irony of the situation.	What is ironically funny here?
	Take deep abdominal breaths and count to 12.	What will I let go of?
	Think of someone worse off than you.	Who would love to switch places with me?
	Say, "Oh well, big deal, so what, who cares." in order, three times fast.	How much of my energy and emotion does this situation really deserve?

(Note: this is NOT an exhaustive list of ways to f yourself, but it will get you started.)

Baby shi*f*t first

Start small with this.
Baby steps.
At first, you'll be *f*'ing yourself
when you are faced with things like:

> Moody friends, bad hair,
> lame classes, a dead
> cell phone, arriving late,
> fender benders, bullying,
> boring teachers, over-
> sleeping, and low grades.

Doing so will make a huge difference in your life.
All these baby shi*f*ts will collectively change your life so much
that it will shock the shi*f*t out of you.

W hen you nail this at its foundational level, you will be much more equipped to apply it to virtually anything life throws you.

Take your time with this.

We're not suggesting that you apply this concept to some big tragic issue in your life right out of the gate.

This shifting process is best done at a micro level *first*, then *later* you can apply it at the macro level for things like: broken hearts, death, illness, parental divorce, failing a class, rejection from college, and other life-changing events.

It's kind of like needing your first grade alphabet lesson before you can conquer the periodic table.

So go easy on yourself. This is a process. You have to crawl before you walk.

Oh, and it's not a race. It's your life.

Examples anyone?

CRAPPY SITUATION: Your parents inform you that you'll be babysitting your little sister on Friday night.

OBSERVE AND RESIST the knee-JERK reaction to vent your frustration and shout how unfair it is.

SAY: "Oh, shi*f*t!"

CHOOSE: *f*IND the benefit.

ASK: How could this actually benefit me?

ANSWER: If I scratch my parents back, maybe they'll scratch mine and let me borrow the car next weekend.

RESULT: You coolly reply with "No problemo!"

And the award for Sibling of the Year goes to....

CRAPPY SITUATION: Your English teacher assigns an essay one week before semester finals.

OBSERVE AND RESIST the knee-JERK reaction to stress out and worry about how you're going to get it all done in such a short amount of time.

SAY: "Oh, shi*f*t!"

CHOOSE: *f*LIP *your belief / opinion*

ASK: What belief or opinion would serve me better?

ANSWER: If I do this now I can stop stressing about it.

RESULT: You bee-line it to the computer lab and knock out a great essay.

Mega-cool.

CRAPPY SITUATION: Your friend Katie cancels lunch plans with you for the umpteenth time.

OBSERVE AND RESIST the knee-JERK reaction to take it personally and rip her a new one.

SAY: "Oh, shi*f*t!"

CHOOSE: *f*IND the truth.

ASK: What information am I lacking?

ANSWER: When you ask Katie why she keeps breaking plans with you, she confides in you that lately her parents can't afford to give her any allowance and she was too embarrassed to tell you.

RESULT: A clear reminder that it's not always about you. And you avoid hurting Katie when she needs a friend. Whew!

This is the power behind the *f*'in shi*f*t.

CRAPPY SITUATION: You sprain your ankle a day before the biggest school dance of the year.

OBSERVE AND RESIST the knee-JERK reaction to have a pity party for yourself.

SAY: "Oh, shi*f*t!"

CHOOSE: *f*REAK. Laugh at the irony of the situation.

ASK: What is ironically funny here?

ANSWER: Duh!

RESULT: You make a t-shirt that says **"May I have this ~~dance~~ limp?"** and wear it to the dance.

Are you getting
the hang of this?

Thank you?

Year... 2008
Place... Portland, OR
Lesson...Gratitude rocks

I was stopped for speeding (80 in a 55) and I was so sosoosoooo angry at myself. I was so mad, it was difficult for me to resist my knee-JERK reaction in the moment (banging my fists on the steering wheel and yelling obscenities).

I *hate* getting in trouble. (Never mind that I'm breaking the law.)

As I watched the officer approach my car from my rearview mirror, I started to feel resentment toward him.

Enter my Ego:

"What a crappy job to have. Doesn't he feel bad pulling people over all day? How does he sleep at night knowing he has ruined so many people's days?"

I was clearly pissed off —at him.

Luckily though, I was smart enough to know that an attitude like that wouldn't get me far with the law (or in life).

So, in true shi*f*thead form, I tried hard to *observe* and *resist*.

Then, of course, I said, "Oh, shi*f*t!"

I t was right around Thanksgiving, and I tried to have an attitude of gratitude. Before I knew it, I was rolling down the window and listening to myself say the words:

"Thank you, officer."

Yep, I thanked the guy for pulling me over. And yes, he was as shocked as I was. But as I listened to myself talk, it made sense.

I was driving too fast, which was dangerous not only to myself but to others. It was this guy's job to keep the road safe, and I was *grateful* for that.

It was almost like an out-of-body experience. I could hear the words, but I couldn't believe I was saying them.

He went back to his car with my license and registration, and I actually felt okay. By taking that *attitude of gratitude* and saying "thank you" out loud to him, I actually calmed myself down.

While the cop was in his patrol car writing up what I figured would be about a $250 citation, I was sitting there thinking how freaking stupid and genius I was all in a span of five minutes.

Not a minute later the cop was at my window...

...handing me a warning.

Unbelievable, I know.

I swear this really happened.

This shift works.

It's so awesome, and so much fun, once you get the hang of it.

Something this fun
should be illegal.

OK, LET'S REVIEW.
This is easy. You've got this.

When you come face-to-face with a crappy situation:

ONE
Observe and resist your knee-JERK reaction.

TWO
Say "Oh, shi*f*t!"

THREE
Choose an appropriate *f* in strategy
to reframe your crappy situation.

FOUR
Ask yourself an *f* in question.

FIVE
Answer it.

SIX
Feel the shi*f*t.

Ahhhhh!

Let's shoot the shift

Put holes in it, if you dare.

So Jen, can anyone be a shi*f*thead?

Sure, this isn't rocket science. However, sometimes, when I tell

potential shi*f*theads about this simple method, they resist and try to shoot holes in the theory to challenge its simplicity. And that's good. I love a challenge.

Mark: Oh, really smarty pants? Then you'll love my student Alex. He may only be sixteen, but he's a veteran skeptic.

Jen: Cool. Bring it on. I know he can shift if he puts his mind to it. It's simple and the results will rock his world!

ALEX: Are you serious? You expect me to believe that just by saying a few words out loud and thinking something different I am going to change my life?

JEN: I don't expect you to believe anything that doesn't feel right to you. I *am* offering up a different way to go about your life. The cool thing is it's your choice.

ALEX: *(in a slightly sarcastic tone)* Fine. Whatever. I'll give it a try.

JEN: Are you sure? Because this won't work if you really aren't into it, or don't believe it. I mean, it would be like an atheist showing up at church on Sunday. And I don't need to tell you how ridiculous that would be. Again, this is your choice, and you get to believe what you want.

ALEX: I get it. Let's get to the problem. There's this really obnoxious guy in my class that annoys the hell outta me. He's a bully and makes rude comments to embarrass me. It drives me nuts and I'm at a point where I can't take much more.

JEN: How does this guy make you feel?

ALEX: What do you think? Pissed off!

JEN: So is it safe to assume you want something different from that part of your life experience?

ALEX: Yeah.

JEN: And do you commit to doing something different than what you have been doing?

ALEX: Now, *this* sounds like church.

JEN: Well it *is* a philosophy with a pretty strong following…

ALEX: Okay, fine. I commit to doing things differently.

JEN: And are you willing to submit yourself to the process and try on new ways of thinking and doing so you can get different results?

ALEX: Uh huh.

JEN: Now I've got to give you some tough love. You have to face the fact that the people of the world are not here to serve *you*. And you can't make them. You have no control over what others do and say. None.

ALEX: Wait a minute. I didn't say I wanted people to serve me. I just want them to be different so they're not so annoying.

JEN: You want other people to be different? How long have you been trying to hike that hill? People are who they are. They show up in your life exactly the way they're supposed to. You can't control anything except the way you react to them. They're annoying because you have defined them that way. If you say they're annoying, they will be annoying. You get to determine your reality. And until you face that truth you can do nothing to change it.

ALEX: Geez. That's heavy, but I'm tracking.

JEN: Right on. So, here is where you get to shift the situation and get your power back. Remember, whenever you let yourself react negatively to the way someone is being, you have given up your power to them. Relinquished it. Handed it over. You are letting them control you. So by choosing to see the situation differently, you never give it up, you are always in control. And you *so* deserve that.

ALEX: I'm listening.

JEN: First, I invite you to say the two magic words.

ALEX: Oh, shi*f*t!

JEN: Nice. You are halfway to shi*f*ting the situation and getting your power back. Funny what one little "f" can do, huh?

ALEX: Mmm. We'll see.

JEN: Now go *f* yourself.

ALEX: What???

JEN: Refer back to your list of crafty moves that will help you react differently. Remember, *f*LIP, *f*IND and *f*REAK.

ALEX: OK, *f*LIP.

JEN: Now choose what you want to *f*LIP. Your focus? Your expectations? Your feelings? Your opinion? What?

ALEX: Well, I can't change my opinion about him. He's a rude jerk and that's that.

JEN: Apparently we should start there.

ALEX: How do you expect me to change my opinion about a guy I know is 110% pure moron?

JEN: Well, you could start with telling your Ego to pipe down. You can recognize that he's not exactly the kind of person you would hang out with, but thinking of him as a moron is, as you said, "driving you nuts". It doesn't seem like this belief is serving you at all. Now, choose different words to describe him. What is the opposite of moronic and rude?

ALEX: I don't know. Smart and nice?

JEN: Good. What's this guy's name?

ALEX: Brian

JEN: You are going to fLIP your belief about Brian by changing the words you use to describe him.

ALEX: What? Like saying that Brian is smart and nice? Yeah right! No way. He's so not smart *or nice.*

JEN: Alright, if you say so.

ALEX: This is really stretching it now. If you knew this guy you would agree with me. Brian is like the biggest loser I know.

JEN: Actually, I wouldn't agree with you, because in doing so I would be setting myself up for disappointment, frustration, anger and pain every time I saw Brian. And I'm just not that into self-sabotage and emotional mutilation. But it sounds like you are. So are you willing to submit to this process and try something new, or not?

ALEX: Geez. Tough crowd. Fine…Brian is smart and nice.

JEN: Now say it like you mean it.

ALEX: Brian is smart and nice!

JEN: Good, now let's add a little *f*REAK. Say it again but with a big smile on your face.

ALEX: This is ridiculous.

JEN: Look, you have two choices in life. You get to choose **happy** or **crappy**. I am fine if you choose crappy, but don't come complaining to me about it. I know better. I know that you can live happily by simply changing your perspective and getting control of your thoughts and actions. That way you can get different results - and be happy! Let me help you with this one. Tell me something that Brian is actually good at.

ALEX: Umm…He's a decent swimmer.

JEN: Good. What else?

ALEX: Well, I hate to admit it but he's a great guitar player. I actually heard one of his songs and it was pretty good.

JEN: Cool. What else.

ALEX: Isn't that enough?

JEN: What else is Brian good at?

ALEX: He dresses okay, I guess.

JEN: Good. Now tell me about Brian and do it with a smile.

ALEX: Brian is a guy I go to school with who is a decent swimmer, a good guitar player and a good dresser.

JEN: How does that feel?

ALEX: Unnatural. Uncomfortable. Ridiculous.

JEN: Perfect! When anything feels uncomfortable that means you are stretching and growing.

JEN: Say it again.

ALEX: Brian is a guy I go to school with who is a decent swimmer, a good guitar player and a good dresser!

JEN: More creative with your language. Add some *f*REAK!

ALEX: Brian is a guy I go to school with who's an awesome swimmer, a rockin guitar player and a super cool dresser.

JEN: That was ridiculously freaky. But you obviously get the point. Now how do you feel when you think about Brian?

ALEX: Better actually. At least for now. Although when I see him again I'm sure all those original feelings will come back.

JEN: What can you do to stay in this mindset when you see him next?

ALEX: I guess I could say this weird statement again to myself.

JEN: Good idea. Then when you've got that down you can graduate to actually saying it out loud to someone else. Now, that's cool. And if you really want to take control of your life you can one day aspire to tell Brian directly to his face! Imagine that.

Alex: I think I'll start with me for now.

JEN: That is the smartest thing I've heard you say all day.

So, how will Alex change his life once he gets the hang of this?

Great question.

When he starts to control the way he reacts to things that happen in his daily life by *f*'in himself with a *f*LIP, *f*IND or *f*REAK, he'll start to recognize the benefits it brings him and he'll be hooked.

Once he's hooked he'll want to do more and more of it. He'll be looking for ways to shi*f*t every situation.

It will be like a really fun game that he always wins. This is the moment Alex will go from being a Potential Shi*f*thead to being a Bona Fide Shi*f*thead.

It is the insistent and consistent effort
that transforms him from
a wanna-be to the real deal.

H

ere are a few of the rewards that this shifthead gets to reap:

✓ He will feel happier and more positive, which will be so attractive to others they will be drawn to him like mosquitoes to a bug light.

✓ He'll have more friends.

✓ He'll be more independent.

✓ He'll get more of what he wants.

✓ He'll be more relaxed and confident.

✓ He'll be in control of his life.

The benefits are endless.
It's a snowball effect,
and it all starts with saying
the words…Oh, shift!

When the shift hits the fan

Inevitable roadblocks and resistance.

I magine for a moment that you are Pac Man.

Yes, Pac Man.

You're chugging along, at a nice speed, enjoying the ridiculous electronic music in the background with a big cheesy grin on your big yellow head.

Life is good.

And then you see them. In the distance, these freaking ghost monsters all start coming toward you at once. You take a left and they go left. You head toward the corner and they follow.

They are on you like white on rice, and their mission is to gobble you up. They don't like the beat to which you are dancing. You are ruining everything for them and they want you stopped—dead. They were just fine until your smiley ass came around and caused them to stir.

Oh, and they are mad, at least they look mad. I mean what do they have to be happy about? They were pretty much pro-grammed to be pissed off by default and to gobble up anyone that looks or acts differently than them.

And you do.

Look at you. Dancing around, eating up all the frickin' dots and fruit, and achieving high scores like your shift doesn't stink.

Look at *them*. They don't even have a mouth to smile with, just a shifty set of eyes, peeking out from behind their colorful (protective) moo moos.

H ere comes the ugly truth…

Brace yourself.

These ghost monsters are your friends and family who CAN'T HANDLE YOUR SHI*f*T!

Not ALL your friends and family. Just the ones that CAN'T HANDLE YOUR SHI*f*T!

They love you. They really do, and they want the best for you. The problem is that some of them think the "best" is the route *they're* taking. So when you deviate from what everyone else is doing, they want to bring you back with the pack. Where it's "normal".

But remember…

Normal ≠ Good

Now, it's not like these people are consciously setting out to envenom you with their negative thinking and grim outlook on life. They don't mean to do harm. This is just how they are and, up until now, so were you.

Then you decided to shi*f*t.

f'in yourself all over the place. Holding yourself responsible for the way you react to life. You are *f*lipping, *f*inding, *f*reaking, and all is going well.

And one day (more or less)…

…you show up like the shi*f*thead you are

and they notice that you…

refuse to join in on their gossip rants,

react with grace instead of anger when things don't go your way,

stop complaining about the trivial,

insist on finding the silver lining,

compliment instead of criticize,

laugh instead of cry…

And they respond with...

"What the hell is going on?"

"What happened to you?"

"I'm not sure I like this."

Why would they? Most of them haven't searched deep within themselves for truth, or worked hard at changing their lives by changing the way they react.

They may not know you are on this path, wanting and working for change.

They *do* know *you*. Or at least they *did* know you the way you used to be, and they liked you that way.

They may have even liked you *because* you were that way *(gossipy, angry, egocentric, complaining, judgmental, negative, mean, high-strung—fill in the blank with your own special words).*

Now what are they supposed to do

...with you?

This is when the shift hits the fan.

When some of your friends and family see you in full shifthead form they may start to feel a disconnect.

But not all of them…

You'll know the ones that feel disconnected by the confused and slightly disappointed look on their face when you start to re-act differently to life.

Some people will not be able to handle your shift, and at that point you have a choice. You can either sink under their pressure and go back to your old reality, OR you can stand strong and stay shifted.

Ask yourself:

Who do you want to make happy?
Who deserves to hold your power?
Who is meant to control your life?
Who do you have to answer to?

Them or you?

The choice is yours and it will test your resolve.

It's a good thing
you are so powerful
and mighty.

Alarmed

Year... 1991
Place... New Jersey
Lesson... Tell'em

When I was on a visit home from first year of college, my mother and I were leaving to go shopping. I had forgotten about the sensitivity of our home security system and how it all worked. In my careless forgetfulness I accidentally set off the alarm. Not your ordinary alarm, but one that calls in the fire trucks and police cars simultaneously, which in our small town was a big deal.

My mother was livid, but not because I set off the alarm; after all, accidents happen. She was pissed because I failed to choose the

OH-MY-GOD-THE-SKY-IS-FALLING

reaction that I had chosen in the past, one that I clearly learned from her. When my reaction was more like OH-WELL-BIG-DEAL, one that I had clearly learned at college, she laid into me.

In all fairness she was justified, kind of.

I mean, that's how I had reacted in the past, and now that I wasn't reacting in the same way, she was confused...and pissed.

And I was bummed. Really bummed.

What I learned that day (and have obviously never forgotten) is that if you're going to shi*f*t, you have to realize that it will impact others around you in ways that may not be agreeable.

It's at that moment you have a decision to make.

That day I considered putting on my drama hat to appease my mother—to give her what she very much needed from me. I love her dearly and I wanted to please her, but I couldn't.

It was no longer in me.

I wasn't who I had been.

I had shi*f*ted.

So instead I cried like a baby. I cried because I could feel the tension, resistance and pure disappointment in my mother for me not "being" the way she knew me to be. The way I used to be. Oh, and it sucked.

I am, however, very glad that I didn't give in and show up as the drama queen I left home as. It was painful, but I stuck with it.

In hindsight, I probably should have given my mother the heads-up she deserved and told her that it's not that I didn't care; I just didn't want to make mountains out of molehills anymore.

This was my shift and I really wanted to own it.

Instead, I assumed she would understand me and all the changes I had made while I was away.

Don't do that.

Let people know you are on this path so it doesn't hit them upside the head.

It's a nice gesture.

Scared shiftless

Literally.

It feels like I work so hard just to fit in, yet I'm always in doubt whether it's working. Half the time I wish I could be invisible, just so I could finally relax. I live as though people are constantly judging the way I look and act, but maybe it's really only me judging myself. I want to change the way I think so badly. But is it even possible?

James, 15

You are sooo not alone, James?
And yes, it's sooo possible.

YOU

are your own worst enemy when it comes to change. Actually, it's not all of you, it's your Ego. And it's fugly.

It rules your Self through fear.

It's true.

Fear keeps us from happiness, love, achievement, and all the other things we most want in life.

And fear can definitely keep us from shifting.

The top 5 fears

that keep teens from shifting.

Are you ready for this?

Fear #1

I will lose my identity. I won't be entertaining, witty or funny anymore. I will be boring.

I'm always cracking people up at school. I usually get the most laughs when I'm making fun of someone. It's hilarious and people love it.

Andrew, 16

No they don't. They think you're a bully and are probably too afraid to say anything in fear of being your next target. Fun doesn't have to come at the expense of others. Funny is also possible without being negative. If your Ego has been doing stand-up for most of your life, it's not funny. It's rude.

Think of someone who is entertaining, witty and funny without making others look bad. Wouldn't you want to be his/her friend?

Fear #2

I will lose some of my friends.

Yes you will. And thank goodness for that. Were they really friends to begin with? The people who are attracted to you for your Ego-driven ways are the same ones that will fall off when you shift.

Take stock. Who in your life needs to be flushed out?

In our research for this book, one PSH told me:

> *When I decided to stop gossiping with my friends, Sara and Patrice, they started to get pissy and said I was being lame. It made me super sad to know that I couldn't be myself around my "friends". Now I hang around people who aren't such downers. I feel way better about myself and have friends who like me for me.*
>
> *Claire, 18*

Be wary of friends who think gossiping, complaining and whining is FUN. What does that say about them? Better yet, what does that say about *you* having *them* as your friends?

Double ouch.

Fear #3

People will think I'm a goodie-two-shoes.

When you are lying on your deathbed,

will you be wishing

you were known

as a jerk

or a

really

nice

person?

Fear #4

I'll be a pushover and lose my edge.

This is another good one. You may think if you squash out the Ego you will surrender the social skills, winning mentality or competitive edge that you "need" to get ahead.

Read this great Aesop fable, and then decide if brutal force is the only way to get what you want.

THE WIND AND THE SUN

The Wind and the Sun were disputing which was stronger. Suddenly they saw a traveler coming down the road, and the Sun said, "I see a way to decide our dispute. Whichever of us can cause that traveler to take off his cloak shall be regarded as the stronger. You begin." So the Sun retired behind a cloud, and the Wind began to blow as hard as it could upon the traveler. But the harder he blew, the more closely the traveler wrapped his cloak around him, until at last the Wind had to give up in despair. Then the Sun came out and shone in all his glory upon the traveler, who soon found it too hot to walk with his cloak on.

"KINDNESS AFFECTS MORE THAN SEVERITY."

Fear #5

I will fail at this.

F ail? Are you kidding? Of course you'll fail.

Mark Twain wrote, *"Quitting smoking is easy. I've done it a thousand times."* Remember, shifting takes an insistent and consistent effort. Don't expect to arrive all at once. Just keep your head down, stay focused and know that each situation presents another opportunity to succeed.

Stay in the moment and set your intention on making this one change in your life.

The only way you can really fail is if you *fail to try*—again and again.

Being a shi*f*thead means being a fighter, a worker bee, a disciple of your Self – a tenacious human who is conscious about how you view your world and consistent in shifting the views that don't serve you.

And remember, you can't go on autopilot here. You never get to quit. It's kinda like learning.

And we know you love that.

Get your shift together

Just the FAQ's.

Jen, how are we supposed to shift when there's so much negativity in the world?

Turn off the *freakin'* news.

Like food for your body, the news feeds your brain. Watching the news is equivalent to eating a Big Mac. It does nothing but fill you up with crap.

It might feel good going down, but the consequences are brutal. Just don't do it. Cut yourself off from the news. Tell yourself it's cancerous… 'cause it's that deadly.

Now, I am not suggesting you cut yourself off completely and become an apathetic citizen.

You know the crap news I am referring to.

I guarantee you that hearing about who got hit by a car, murdered, raped or shot does not make you an "informed citizen", or help you in any way.

Turn. It. Off.

You'll be so glad you did.

Mark: How can teens shift when the people they hang out with are so negative?

Jen: If you are surrounded by people who live in a negative space, let them own it as theirs not yours. Allow them to be where they are and don't agree to join them.

Honoring people where they are is the best gift you can give them—just insist on receiving the same respect from them.

Let the sh*theads in your life know that you are no longer willing to play in their sandbox. They can be there till they rot if they want to, but they can't drag you back in it, no matter how lonely they get in there. It's your responsibility to tell them this. You can't assume they will get it without being told.

Set your boundaries
and let them know about it...

And another thing.

Being a shifthead is the greatest way to clean house and get rid of the bad apples that bring you down.

Those toxic, stinky types that cause you more grief than you deserve…

You know who I am talking about.

Let them go.

Mark: Is it really that easy?

Jen: No way. I'm not suggesting it's easy. If it were, you and I would have done it by now. And so would everyone else.

But if anyone needs some convincing, I tell 'em to chew on this:

- Discomfort is a necessary evil and a sure sign that you are on a path toward change.

- Do what you've always done and you'll always get what you've always gotten.

- Letting people know that you have taken back control of your life is a gutsy thing to do. Letting them go is even gutsier. But you've guts – so use 'em.

- You deserve to be surrounded by people who feed your soul, not suck it dry.

- You always have a choice. Always.

> I'm not saying you have to do this. I'm just thinking you might want to.☺

Mark: How can we get people we care about to shi*f*t?

Jen: Here's what you do...

Give a shi*f*t. But just one.

As a shi*f*thead your radar is always on. You can't help it. You will start to pick up on others' negative reactions and self-defeating behavior. It will be blaring, actually.

As a result, you will want to show others the light, and you should. **But just once.**

Be willing to show people how they could view their crappy situation from a different perspective, or how they might react in a different way to get a different result.

Get them to *f*LIP, *f*IND and *f*REAK by asking them powerful questions. Giving people the chance to change their lives is a charitable act that everyone deserves to receive.

Don't 'ya think?

N ow, here's the important part…

When you begin to show them the power of shifting, observe their response to your generous gift. If they are receptive and seem to really tune in to what you're sharing, they are probably open to more. Cool.

If not, back off.

You can't force people to jump on your gravy train. If they're not ready, you can't *make* them shift.

Mark: What are we supposed to do with the people who don't want to shift?

Jen: Nothing. Simply continue to walk and talk like your shift doesn't stink. Just show up in the best way that makes you happy, knowing that's all you can do. Stand strong in the belief that this is the right path for you; and if your friends or loved ones want to join you, they will.

It's that simple.

Trust me; you don't want to be like one of those hyped-up vegetarians or religious converts who are so adamant about getting you to do it "their way". That's such a huge turn-off.

Those people make me want to eat a steak and join a cult.

But there are others who don't try to suck you in, they just live and let live. You know the type. They simply do their thing and could care less if you notice it or not. If you notice, and it's attractive to you, perhaps you'll follow suit. If you don't notice, then it's not meant to be on your radar at that time.

A nyway you slice it, people are more prone to take action when the action isn't being shoved down their throats. Just be your fabulous self. Those who are ready will follow.

That's the way it will be when you show up like a shifthead. Those who like what they see will be open to receiving your help. Those who aren't will resist following your lead. And that's perfectly fine.

Show them the way and let them decide. The good news is that *shiftheaditis* is contagious. People will start to see your life changing virtually overnight, and they'll be wondering what you're on.

When they do, just pass 'em a copy of this book.

We'll have them at hello.

That's good shift

You are the Shift

This is about YOU changing your life.

YOU, the shifthead, coming to

terms with the fact that YOU

have complete control

of your life

starting

right

now.

And that's good.

Real good.

What will that control get you?

One thing.

The one and only thing you really want.

It's what you are here to experience.
It's what you were born into.

Your natural birthright...

JOY

Joy is yours.

All yours.
If you choose it.

Once you learn this.

The moment you embrace this single truth.

When you make this shi*ft*…

You are *f*ree.

Free from the prison of victimhood.
Free from pain and suffering.
Free from your Ego.
Free from confusion, indecision and regret.
Free from self-limiting beliefs.
Free from self-doubt, blame and judgment.

And with that comes the freedom to be
who you are and live the life you desire.
The freedom to celebrate
your victories and failures equally.
You are free to succeed at anything.
You are free to find JOY wherever you look.
Simply because you choose to.

When you make this shi*ft* so many *f*'in things
are going to change in your life you
won't even know what hit 'ya.

You will be happier.
You will feel powerful.
You will *be* powerful.
You will be a positive influence.
You'll attract more quality people, experiences and opportunities in your life.
Your health will improve.
Your relationships will improve.
You'll get better grades.
You'll get a job.
You'll like your job.
You'll get a date.
You'll be more likeable to your date.
You'll bounce out of bed in the morning.
You will get what you want.
You will laugh more.
You will worry less.
You'll avoid disease.
You'll sleep better.
You'll make more friends.
Your life will have more meaning.
You will like yourself.
You'll be liked by others.
You'll exercise more.
You'll lose weight. *(Individual results may vary.)*

You'll glow.
You'll be more sane.
You'll cry less.
Your skin will clear up.
You'll discover new things.
You will see the light.
You'll avoid the dark.
Your parents will be proud.
You'll be better looking.
You'll smell better. (Really.)
You'll like, maybe love, your life.
Your reputation will improve.
You'll live a more authentic life.
You'll model the behavior you hope to see in others.
Your younger siblings will learn from the best.
You'll make people smile.
You'll breathe easier.
You'll be more successful.
You'll be admired and envied (in a healthy way).
You'll wear less black.
Your phone will ring more.
You'll have more energy.
You'll have fewer regrets.
You will be infectious.
You will make a difference.
You will positively contribute to the good of the universe.

You deserve this.

We love you.
We know that sounds freakin' weird, but if you haven't noticed,
we don't talk smack or say shift we don't mean.

It's true.

And if we can love you,
then you can love yourself enough
to get off your butt and change your life.
This is your life we're talking about here.
Oh, and it's not like Costco where you get to buy endless
amounts in bulk-size quantities.
You just get this one little, neatly packaged,
limited-time-only life.

Stop acting like it's disposable.

There really is no more where this came from.
Therefore, you deserve to have every single day filled with
joy, peace and success.
And it's all within your control.
Do you get that?
You were born as this little superhero
with the biggest superpower of them all.
The power to choose.

Wham! BadaBOOM! Ka-POW!

It's a movement

Be a part of it.

So....

You've made the shift.

You choose JOY.

Now every decision you make, every reaction you select, every perspective you adopt will come from that place, and will simultaneously lead you there.

How?

Whenever you choose
        to start from joy
                you inevitably end up there.

Full circle, baby.

You are so cool.

And when you're that cool, you have a job to do.

Your job is to share this with others.
That's right. Don't keep it to yourself.
It's too good, and so are you.

Your light is shining so bright you couldn't hide it if you tried.

We dare you to be a star in someone's life.
Guide them.
Show them what they can be.
Tell them it's as simple as making a choice.
Tell them about the one little letter.
Let them know that life
doesn't have to be anything less than amazing.
Remind them of their natural birthright
and tell them that they too
deserve to be on this

JOY RIDE

called

LIFE.

Choose JOY
and light the path
for others to do the same.

That's what shiftheads do.

This isn't just about you. It's about us.

All of us working together to create a shift
so big that it makes a mark on the world.

*(Seriously, we're not exaggerating
about the world part.)*

You
and
Us.

Making a mark on the world.

You can do this.

We believe in you.
You have all you need to take
this small step towards big change.
Just start by saying two simple words.
If you can't say it, you can't do it.
And we *know* you can say it.

You are a rock star and your potential is colossal.
Bigger than you can imagine.
Don't waste it.
Honor it.
Say it.
Be it.

"Oh, shi*f*t!"

ACKNOWLEDGEMENTS

Our teen shiftheads: Risa Luther, Zoe Chrisman-Miller, Olivia Jones-Hall, Aidyn Smith, Robin Liu, Tommy Burke, Caitlyn McLain, Sydney Confer, Kess Mann, Julia Espinosa, Kyra Mygrant, Zach Padaca and Fedor Polyakov.

Susan Anglada Bartley, M.Ed. for her editing genius and her commitment to teaching our youth.

Vikki Mueller-Espinosa for her support and dedication to helping get the *Oh, shift!* message out to the world.

All the adult shiftheads who are out there doing their part. Keep it up… teens are watching.

ABOUT THE AUTHORS

Jennifer Powers is a fearless, loving heart who insists on making a difference in the world before she checks out. She coaches, speaks and writes from a place of honesty, service and pure giddiness. She is a believer in the human spirit; her mission is to help others find their truth, whatever that may look like. And whether she has met you yet or not, she is your biggest fan.

Oh, and when Jennifer does meet you…
expect a hug.

Reach out to her at Jennifer@jenniferpowers.com

Mark Tucker is today's up and coming teen expert. Over the past decade, he's connected with thousands of teens discussing their thoughts, needs, and challenges while empowering them to trust their voice and own their truth.
He listens, understands, and supports teens at a time when they need it the most.

And when you meet Mark, get ready to laugh your butt off.

Give him a shout at Mark@NlivenYou.com

Dog Shift.

Jennifer loves dogs.
Actually, she loves all animals.

That's why part of the proceeds from
this book will be donated to
The Humane Society of the United States
www.hsus.org

Woof.

One last thing...

Thank you for being so f 'in beautiful.

Believing in you,
Jennifer & Mark

NOTES

NOTES

NOTES

NOTES

NOTES

NOTES

NOTES

NOTES

NOTES

NOTES